STREET CAKE

experimental writing prize

winners' anthology

2020

EDITED BY

NIKKI DUDLEY

&

TRINI DECOMBE

Published in the United Kingdom in 2020
by streetcake magazine
124 Cadogan Terrace, London, E9 5HP.

First printing, 2020

ISBN 978-1-8380-9600-7

Cover design by Trini Decombe
Typesetting by Alec Newman Book Design
alecnewman.kfs@gmail.com

contents

foreword

We are extremely happy to have been able to deliver our experimental writing prize for the second time in 2020, building on the successes of the first year and also learning a lot in order to move forward and grow. None of us expected 2020 to be quite so challenging but one of the good things for us is that we have been working hard to continue developing a network of organisations, judges and writers who are as passionate about the prize as we are!

We've begun to notice that more and more people understand the term 'experimental' and are sending us an amazing range of work, which was also true for the prize. Choosing was not an easy task for us! We want everyone to know that we appreciate you trusting us with your work and we are so pleased you wanted to be involved with our prize.

The longlisted and shortlisted writers also deserve huge recognition and they should not forget that they took huge strides just by entering, and we hope they'll be back another year to grab a placed spot!

The prize has seen some development this year. The first change is expanding our anthology to include four top placed writers instead of three. We are also offering mentoring to the second placed writers, which will be delivered by ourselves. We hope this will expand the opportunities for development to writers and give them more sustained support. Moreover, we will be expanding the networking/exhibition and performance opportunities. We want people to know this is not just a one-off prize, it's a development programme.

This year, we would also like to acknowledge the support of all the organisations who shared news of the prize and supported our work. 2020 saw us offer sponsored places to many writers, some of whom are in this anthology and many others who appreciated a helping hand to enter the prize. We want to champion diversity within the writing we publish and the writers we work with.

We can't wait for you to enjoy the range of innovative and emotive work we have for you this year. We're really proud of all the writers included and we hope you'll be seeing a lot more of them and their writing!

We also want to thank ACE for funding this project and being understanding in these challenging times. Our judges have all been incredibly helpful and supportive as ever: Sascha Akhtar, Nik Perring,

Jarred McGinnis and Astra Papachristodoulou. Big thanks also to: Isabelle Kenyon and Fly on the Wall Press, Haley Jenkins and Selcouth Station Press, SJ Fowler, Writers' Centre Kingston, Leone Ross, Joe Ruddock, Simon Cusack, Alec Newman of KFS Press, Untitled Writing, Hive South Yorkshire, Sam Ruddock, Laura Kenwright, James Trevelyan, Spread the Word, and everyone else who has supported our work and sent us good vibes throughout.

We hope you enjoy the writing in this anthology as much as we do. Thank you for reading.

Nikki and Trini

Managing Editors, streetcake.

FICTION
18 - 23

school night

I think the doctor will tell me that I have a puncture in my brain. This stuff leaks. The juice of it jellies the meat of me like wet dog food. I bloat with it.

She wears the silver necklace even to bed. The earrings and hair clips ask after it from the mirrored jewellery dish on the dresser.

'C' it says - the necklace charm. Her first initial. C, et cetera.

I try her name in my mouth and feel it sink right through. Bits of bone wobble and clack in the aspic where my gut used to be: c-c-c-c-c-c-c-c-c

She turns slow onto her back and holds her phone out between pink-lacquered thumbs.

Facebook Messenger lights a square of bright country in the duvet, where I might go to start a new life. A little of that pissy fake-tan smell and a recently blown-out vanilla bean candle. The waning moon shivers in the folds of a Topshop pyjama vest.

can you send me the homework from yesterday?

yeah sure x

cool :) gn xx

night x

Her parents are still awake across the landing. I can hear the radio, just.

Her cold foot touches my leg over the sheet and I stick like one of those dolls in a birthday cake skirt. The things she might say, the film of strange toothpaste on her tongue. I listen, wait for sirens in the street outside the petrol station.

My skin might never be so smooth, so soft again.

it hurts

i.

I heard you

come in at quarter to three, pour a glass of water, try to be quiet as you try not to fall.

I heard your jeans and heavy belt hit the carpet, a breath out as you pull your top over your head. I know exactly what it looks like even though it's dark.

You lay down next to me.

I feel the warmness of your alcohol breath as your fingers pull me in. The warmth. Your lips on my forehead.

Your breathing eases into sleep.

It is dark.

Your sleep eases into her name.

Her name

in our bed. In my sheets. In this place. As your heavy alcohol breath

You were always bad at keeping secrets, that's why I trusted you.

And now. Now, im about to lose

In my bed. In your arms. Your soft, strong arms god I love your arms, thick and real around my body. Heavy on my rib cage. Your breath in my face and her name again. Again again again again again the word in my head in your arms in this bed and im about to lose my mind I feel it inside. coming up inside. her name. you're lying. I love you

Fuck fuck fuck

ii.

I drag my fingers along your face, the hard edge of your jawline. I feel it inside me. This need, this anger this want to fuck you fuck you fuck you and fuck her and fuck you and fuck you, I'm about to lose my Im about to taste her on you, im about to like it, im about to lose my

Fingertips waking you up slowly.

I slide my other hand from under the pillow, down the skin of your chest, playing with the hair just a little bit, just like you like it. My skin, your skin, slow but hard. My hand around your throat, my hand around your cock.

I have you, in this bed and you are awake now but you won't look me in the eye as I start to move up and down up and down, I see you realise. I see you try not to let me see what you've realised but you were always a bad liar. And up and down now im going to fuck you like a bad liar

I am on top of you

up and down up and down you grimace I pull harder. I know you like it. Bad liar. This is what he likes. And I feel his hand slide up my thigh. Soft. I never liked it soft, but she does.

She likes it soft touch and kissing. Closed eyes lights dimmed fuck her and fuck you for touching me like you touch her. For forgetting how to touch me bad liar fuck you up and down and fuck you up and down and fuck me and fuck you Up and down harder now and you are breathing harder, trying to, I put weight onto your throat see fear up and down I am on top of you thinking about her name and your face turns red and your cock leaks onto my hand fuck me

iii.

You still aren't looking at me

iv.

I let go of your throat I love how you gasp, body shaking moans and try to touch me again.

Not me he wants. But we up and down faster now, he's tensing. Fuck him and fuck her and fuck me fuck me fuck me I think about you all the time. Fuck me fuck me fuck im so wet fuck him and fuck you and fuck you and fuck you fuck I'm about to lose my mind. You're about to cum. I can see it in your right hand and your open mouth.

I love the face you make right before you cum, the clenched fist. My favorite look. I think about you all the time about to cum inside me inside me for me with me. You are so beautiful.

You are so beautiful

You are so beautiful

v.

You look at me now, and you see me looking at you. You see me lick the wet from my hand, you see me spit it onto your cock and you see me up on my knees, above you. you see me say 'fuck me hard like you hate me'

I feel sick

I slide you inside me. Soft and hard I grit my teeth move up and down with you. My knees pushing into the bed I hope I will have bruises in the morning

it creaks but I don't make a sound.

I am thinking up and down, about her. The soft of her lips and the hard of her fake nails and her smell. Peach. Fuck you I cannot get it out of my sheets, for weeks I have slept with him and her

your hand slides up I grab it and force it down. I am breathing harder, heart rate rising, breathing harder, feeling you inside me. hard and soft and I love him god I love him im losing my mind you

are looking me in the eyes. But you are not looking at me

you are not looking at me but

he is looking at me and he is smiling and he likes it and I know he knows I know and he's making me sick I love him I love his cock I'm going to cum and this is good this is good this is what I want, I want him to tell me this is good. The best. I want to make this the best, the best fuck. For him For her For them. So I fuck harder, louder, up and down up and down and grab myself and my leg is cramping but you are nearly there I am nearly there so I keep fucking and the pain spikes up my leg and I love it I love you I love you fuck me harder harder like you hate me yes yes like that like you hate me

vi.

I feel your hand on my throat and I don't stop it. I deserve it

Punish me I'm going to cum for you with you, you inside me. You.

But her too, on his lips, on his tongue, in the heavy alcohol breath, heavy breathing of his body, in the fingers around my throat when I am holding down his arms. He is breathing faster moving faster, fuck me like you hate me, he is inside me I feel him pushing at my edges I can't breathe I am going to cum for him for her for us but I can't breathe I'm going to cum fuck him harder harder harder harder like you hate me harder harder harder please don't make this harder you shudder under me, in me. I feel you cum. Feel your back arch under my thighs I can't breathe you are hot and wet inside me hot hot and wet we are breathing together harder harder he is still inside me still going moving inside me please don't make this harder than it has to be He is making me sick I am going to be sick but I can't do anything but move for him. For him. I can't stay here, I don't want him inside me but I don't want this to stop I want to fuck him to forget her but He can't

I am going to be sick I'm going to cum

I look at his soft stomach, the hair that inches. His back finds the sheets I run my finger along the trail of dark hair finding its way down him and he shudders and gasps to a stop.

vii.

Holding my breath, I let you roll me off and wait for the feeling. The slow way you take it out, letting it touch every bit of my skin, making me feel you leave. I love that. I love you I love you I love you

but you take it out quick. You don't let me feel it like I want to.

you kiss me soft and I can taste her and

I am breathing

you are smiling and I smile. I let you kiss me I feel sick

you get out of bed but it's dark

You stumble and I know this It has happened hundreds of times before. I smile. I love you. It was good. It was good it was good I want you to tell me it was good. Make it good or fuck me again if that's what you need again again again please fuck me again please don't leave the room I can't breathe don't go to the bathroom don't go don't, the fingers are still around my neck.

I watch the skin of your back. I am still choking. Acrylic nails on my throat

viii.

The wet on the bed sheets is cold now, it presses into my thigh I think about the muscles in your chest as you lay down next to me. I will clean the sheets in the morning but they will still smell like peach. Peach

He is already asleep.

I should get up, drink a glass of water wipe away what you left on my legs before it gets something stuck in it.

I'll clean the sheets in the morning

but they will stop smelling of you

they will just smell of peach

and

I want to smell you, tomorrow night before you get home with hot alcohol breath

so I won't clean the sheets tomorrow.

You mumble something that might be my name, but it might be her name and I love you. Fuck I love you so much it hurts

brown bin

Somebody's stolen our bin.

what

Our bin.

its 3am

I know. Do you know how I know? Because I just got home and thought, hey, it's 3am, the bin should've been emptied by now.

I go to the end of the alley and what do I find? It's gone. Stolen.

which bin

Brown.

isnt that for plants
we dont need a plants bin

The pink lid bin is for plants.
The brown bin is for bottles and glass.

cant we order a new one
just ring the council

I don't want a new one, I want ours.
I can't believe someone stole it. What a horrible thing to do.

im going back to sleep

I need to rage at someone. Please be that someone.

fine
you're lucky i dont have work tomorrow
you know it will have been an accident

How can it be an accident? It has our house number in massive letters on the side.

We've been here for years and no one's stolen our bin before.

There was another one there and it hadn't been emptied because they'd put all their bottles in plastic bags. Bet it was them.

so steal theirs

It's full. I don't want a full brown bin.

steal another

And start a bin war?

a bin war could be fun

I don't want to stoop to their level.

look
ill ring the council in the morning
they have to get us a new one

I'm going to send a note.

to the council?

To the bin-stealer.

do you even know who it is

No.
So I guess three streets are getting notes.

thats so sinister
dont do that

How else am I supposed to contact them?

wait until next bin collection and steal it back

We can't wait that long. The note plan is happening.

but if they know youre looking for it theyll never put it back out
and if theyre as spiteful as you they wont care about a note
might steal our other bins
they know our house number
if you send notes everyone will know our house number
i dont want people knocking on complaining about bin drama

What do you care, you're not even here.

i know suburbs and i know that bin drama can last a very long time
i wont be away forever

Yeah.
I don't know. I need to do something.
I've drafted a note.

go on then

"Dear Sir/Madam,

It has come to my attention that someone has taken our brown bin. I assume this was an accident even though our house number is painted very largely on the side, but we would like it back as we are in desperate need of one. Please check your bin and make sure it's yours, and if it isn't, leave it in the alley. We will be watching.

Kind regards,

Number 10 Elizabeth Road."

whats all this "we" and "our"
im not part of this

I'm going to make more.

one for every house?
your hand will cramp

Sometimes justice requires sacrifice.

oh my god
go to bed

I can't go to bed now.
Night shift's sent me nocturnal anyway.

you're not posting them through now are you

As soon as I'm done.

if i got a note like that at 4am id be scared for my life

What's wrong with it?

only psychopaths send notes about stolen bins

What's wrong with the note? It's a nice note.

"we will be watching"?
lovely
you're making us sound like stalkers

Maybe a stalker stole our bin so they can find out what we drink.

evil plan revealed

I bet it was Vanessa. She seems like the type.

how does anyone seem the type to steal a bin

It's the eyes.
Very evil eyes.

vanessas nice
i dont see why you hate her so much

She called my fruitcake better than average.

so what
it is better than average

It's better than that. It's amazing. It won the cake competition two years in a row.

Better than average makes it sound like it's just okay.

It's that type of fake compliment, you know? When someone wants to sound nice but they don't actually mean it.

i like your fruitcake

Did you eat the slice I packed for you?

yeah i had it on the train
thanks

No worries.
Are you okay?

yeah
working hard

Or hardly working.

or working hard
but the pays good and i might get a bonus
so

When are you coming back?

soon

How soon is soon?

soon enough that youll still be going on about this stupid bin

I never let go of anything.
I need one before you come back, no one goes through milk like you.

ive not had any since i got here
local shop doesnt sell it

Scandal. Call the police.
Speaking of, do you think the police would investigate if I told them someone stole our bin?

blue bin, maybe
no one cares about brown bins

I do.

i can see that
i have to go
i need to be up in three hours and we cant all be nocturnal

But I want to keep talking.

sorry, ok?
ill ring the council tomorrow and theyll send a new bin

I don’t care about that.

someones changing their tune
ill phone you in the evening

Okay.
Should I post the notes?

if you want
bit of fun
get our bin back, brave warrior!

Yeah.
That’s what I want home.

heaven.exe_/run/

You wake up.

It's late; the morning light has shifted. Bright white to a hazy yellow and it is gently drifting through the curtains.

Next to you is a lamp and, next to that, a pair of large, round glasses. Like your dad used to wear, you think.

In the kitchen, half a dozen family members crunch on toast and fresh fruit, eggs are cooking on the hob. You're handed a plate – a team effort, they tell you – and you pick up a knife and fork, eager.

The park is a little wet from the day before, but it doesn't matter. We can still stand on the swings, billow our chests out in flight! Your hands are awfully cold against the metal chain so you shrink your arms back into your sleeves. Too big, not the right fit, your mother said when you first paraded round the kitchen in your newest purchase. Now, insulating your hands from the icy metal, you smirk to yourself. *Still not the right fit, huh?* But you know, were she here to see you, she would have swallowed her pride with a smile and admitted her admiration for the ingenious child she made.

At the cinema, you join up with your friends. They're laughing, chattering about last week's news that must have passed you by. You know that you're always at home with your friends; comrades crying on shoulders, fellow battle-worn soldiers with chinks in their armour that match your own. You've even kissed four of them. Two in spin the bottle, one on a whim when drunk, and the last tucked away in a closet, pursuing a crush that never was. Things were never awkward afterwards, but you sometimes wonder what could have been.

It's an old movie and your dad smiled when he dropped you off, mentioning how he would so love to see it again. You want to invite him in too but somehow you feel he would be out of place, or he feels you would be embarrassed, or you both presume the thoughts of the other and the car's already pulling away by the time you stop and question it. No matter. He's seen it before. The film is excellent, and you tell him this when you get home. It seems like the right thing to say.

An old boyfriend calls and you talk for a while. You're just friends now but you still enjoy one another's company and he wanted to tell you that he got his first choice at uni. He's moving there in a month. You're happy for him, really, and he says you could come visit if you're free. Right now, you're not sure what you're doing even tomorrow, but surely there'll be some opportunity next year. You make a mental note to try and travel down; you've still got one of his hoodies to return but that's just an excuse really.

After dinner, the pudding is overcooked again and your mother's attempt at another apple pie produces first laughter, then sighs from all present. Your best friend always finishes her plate, too polite to leave a crumb. Your brother eats the filling and nothing else. And when you come to wash up, the custard jug proves stubborn, so you leave it to soak.

Everyone else is watching TV and chatting merrily until long after you go to bed.

You lie down and close your eyes to the world. Black.

You wake up.

It's late; the morning light has shifted. Bright white to a hazy yellow and it is gently drifting through the curtains.

FICTION
24-30

She shows up again one night in November, with bloody knees and a smile that means catastrophe. She is waiting at the place where she used to wait, at the end of my alley beneath the streetlight. She is shivering. The weather is beginning to turn cold in Hanoi.

'Can you be my medicine?' And she holds up the grazed palms of both hands. She had been driving in my neighborhood when a car had knocked her from her scooter.

I lead her by the elbow out of sight of the window of my apartment and then around the corner to the pharmacy. I had told Emily I was going to the shop on the corner to buy a data card for my phone. We buy bandages and a bottle of saline, and I drive us on her scooter to the nearby park.

Can you be my medicine? She has said those words to me before. But I'd forgotten about it, like so much else.

Her face, for example, is one of those tricky faces that looks different in every photograph.

When I'm not with her, I can't remember it. Only the coldness of her hands, the smell of her hair, (with my lips against her ear) her voice as she says the words, 'how to love.'

It's late and the gates to the park are locked, but there is a woman selling iced tea at the side of the road. We sit down on small plastic stools and I begin to clean her cuts. I hold her hand open and pour the liquid carefully over one palm, then the other, like it's holy water or something. Then the same with her left knee, (my hand briefly on the back of her leg) and her right knee, the deeper wound. I press bandages firmly against it and she tries not to gasp.

Finally her foot, which she hadn't even realized was bleeding until just now. I wrap a bandage around that too, and tie it as best as I can. The whole process takes a long time and is difficult with only the light from my phone which she holds delicately in her shaking hurt hands.

At some point during all of this the woman brings tea and says many things, most of which I don't understand.

'She asked if you are American,' says Chan.

I smile politely at the woman and shake my head. 'Khong, Tiếng Anh.' (No, English.)

'She wants to know how long you've been in Vietnam.'

'A long time now.'

'She says you're very handsome.'

'What did she really say?'

'She asked if we were married.'

The woman keeps talking, but I am hardly listening. I'm remembering our meetings from months ago, Chan leaning towards me across a bowl of Pho, beneath the table my foot trapped between both of hers. A cheap and dirty restaurant close to my work. There's a mouse running along a water pipe and I'm terrified that someone I know will come in and see us together. She gazes up at me, and I laugh, and say, 'don't look at me like that.' I cover her eyes with my hand because one moment more and I know I'm a goner.

Over a few weeks we meet many times, always in public places. Coffee shops and parks, or beside West Lake late after dark. She doesn't tell me much but I begin to piece together parts of her life. She has a sister who lives in Japan, and a boyfriend in Hai Phong. He's a police officer and they've been together since high school. Chan is only a nickname. Her real name is Hương, or maybe Huyền, or something else too ordinary. She is studying at the University of Foreign Trade and tutors kids at the weekend.

I ask her what subject she tutors, but she refuses to tell me. I become interested and ask her every time we meet. 'What do you teach? Is it Maths? English? Music?' Usually she says nothing, or simply, 'my secret.' Other times she likes to tease me and says all serious and seductive, 'how to love.'

'Ôi trời ơi,' I push her away from me and she laughs.

All of this was during one of Emily's long absences. She was in Hong Kong, she was in Taipei. It doesn't matter where. She was busy with work. She had not called or messaged for some time. I'd argue this as an excuse if I thought anyone would buy it for a second.

Chan had added me on Facebook, and sent a message saying she wanted to practice her English with a native speaker. The first time I met her we ate bánh xèo, and she had to show me how to crush the shell firmly into the rice paper as I rolled it. 'Don't be weak,' she had said. When she asked me if I had a girlfriend I said no, and I didn't feel guilty at all.

One night by the lake, the air fuzzy with mosquitos. She keeps interrupting me and asking me to repeat words with a short 'o' sound – across, locked, forgot.

'Ah, your voice,' she says, and tries to repeat the words in the way I have said them. For some reason she sounds younger when she's putting on an English accent.

It was the early hours of the morning by then. I hadn't yet kissed her. I remember she said, 'Can I ask you a personal question?'

'Hmm, how personal?'

'How many girls have you loved?'

'Loved?'

'I mean sex.'

'Oh, I don't know.'

'So many?'

'Not so many, but a few. In Europe it's different. I mean the culture – '

'I know,' she said. 'You mean you didn't love them.'

'Not every one, no.'

'So how do you do it?'

'Sex?'

'No! (Laughing) I mean what do you say to the girl? When you want to have sex with her?'

'I don't know. Usually you don't need to say anything.' I am finding it difficult to look at her face so instead I look out at the lights from the buildings reflected in the water. Gentle ripples of colour. 'Maybe I'd say something simple like ... shall we go?'

Chan laughed then, in a way I hadn't heard her laugh before. A shameless cackle that knocked her off balance. Other people, sat around the banks of the lake, were looking over at us. When eventually she recovered, wiping away tears, she looked right at me and said, 'so, shall we?'

Maybe I knew what I was doing from the beginning. And maybe, then, I should have known how it would end – clean and painful, like a broken bone. But knowing probably wouldn't have changed much anyway. It was the beginning of June. The city in summer. I could feel myself coming alive again.

Back then, I was still working at a summer school in the mornings. I would get out at midday, grab a Bánh mì for lunch on my way home, and then crash out in the air conditioned nirvana of my bedroom.

Later, as the sun went down, she would be waiting at the end of the alley, beneath the streetlight. We'd drive somewhere on her scooter and have dinner, and then afterwards maybe I'd take her back to her dorm and walk the few kilometers home, following the lazy curve of the river. But usually at some point in the evening she'd say, all shy, 'Anh, can we go overnight?'

So instead we drive around looking for a cheap hotel. And this is the happiest part. Really.

Hanoi at night and the restoring promise of what's to come. Driving slowly, the cool night air, the dark empty roads. The gentle glow of traffic lights and neon signs. Her hands snaking beneath my t-shirt, cold fingers against my skin. I could spend every night of my life like this.

In a heavy darkness, her mosquito-bitten arms pull me close. Everything about her is unfamiliar and exciting. Even the way she kisses, the words she murmurs, and how her skin is so white it seems to glow. Her unfathomable face shifts in the dark and becomes the faces of other girls I've known like this, or wanted to.

It goes on in this way until August when Chan gets sick. I'm not surprised. It is Dengue season and Chan, always killing me in these crazy short shorts. Always refusing to use mosquito repellent because she says it's bad for her skin.

'Do you want me to bring you some medicine?' I ask. 'Just tell me what you need.'

It's difficult to hear her voice on the phone because I am walking in a busy street and because she has started to cry. 'What did you say?'

'Can you be my medicine?'

So I sit by her bed every day for a week, pressing cold flannels against her burning skin. Bringing her mugs of ginger tea and reading to her from Pride and Prejudice, the only book she owns in English. Her roommates come and go, smiling shyly and barely saying a word.

In breaks in the fever she sleeps and I open my laptop and try to work. But instead I find myself gazing at the parts of her skin covered in a fiery rash. Her neck, her collarbones, her chest gently rising and falling. Mottles of red against white.

When she starts to get better she still texts me every day – 'I need my medicine.' So I keep turning up with boxes of kimbap and dumplings from her favorite Korean restaurant. We eat it while sitting on the floor of her room and afterwards fall asleep together in her tiny bottom bunk, or lie awake and talk about whatever comes into our heads at that moment. Like:

'I'm a big fan of all the men actually. Especially Mr. Wickham. Do I use that phrase right? I'm a big fan of?'

'Yes. But I don't think you're supposed to like Mr. Wickham.'

'But I do. He's so charming and so handsome.'

'I don't remember if it says anywhere that he's handsome.'

'Well he's handsome in my head. Very extremely handsome. Hey, what's funny?'

'You make me laugh. Very extremely.'

'Make you love?'

'Laugh.'

'No. I think you said love.'

I suppose this could have been a kind of beginning, but actually it's nearly the end.

In September I got another job all the way in Hưng Yên, and Chan had university and the IELTS exam to prepare for. We saw each other less often. Then not at all.

Also, Emily had come back by then. We were living together again and things very quickly went back to the way they had been before. We cooked together in the evenings and made playlists of music we both loved. We even made plans to visit her parents in California that Christmas. One night I saw a missed call from Chan on my phone and I had to make an excuse to go outside and call her back. I don't remember much about the conversation, except that we decided that afterwards we wouldn't talk anymore. She sounded sad, but said she was spending most weekends in Hai Phong now and I understood what she meant.

On my birthday Emily and I went with some other friends to a jazz bar in Hoàn Kiếm. Afterwards she posted a picture of the two of us on Facebook with some cute caption and Chan 'liked' it. I realized she had probably known about Emily from the beginning. I stopped thinking very much about Chan, but when I did I wondered why I felt like the one who'd been tricked.

'So what now?'

The old woman is packing up her stall and we stand so she can take away our chairs. I am looking at Chan's face, hoping to remember it better this time.

'Can you drive with your hands like this?' I am holding her wrists, the backs of her hands resting in my palms.

She nods her head. 'It's not far.'

'Can I ask you something?'

'Vâng ạ, of course.'

'What do you teach?'

She smiles. 'Still with this question?'

'Yeah, sorry.'

'I teach English. I didn't want to tell you because I know my English is not good. I thought you'd laugh at me.'

'I wouldn't have laughed at you.'

She leans her forehead against my chest. She is still shivering. I wrap my arms around her.

We stand very still and don't say anything for a long time. The smell of her hair, (with my lips against her ear).

'Shall we go?'

I can feel her start to laugh against me. A car goes past and for a moment it's like the lights coming up at the end of a play.

When I get home Emily is already in bed. I brush my teeth, get undressed and I lie down beside her. She turns over and says, 'you were gone a long time.'

'The store on the corner was closed. I had to walk quite far.' I have stopped being surprised at how easily I lie to her.

'You're cold.'

I press my hand against her stomach. She gasps and calls me an asshole, but doesn't take my hand away. I pull her closer to me, and if she's surprised at how hard I hold on to her she doesn't say so. I lie awake for a long time, listening to her soft anchoring breaths, and to the sound of the wind outside, starting to stir up dust and debris in the street.

there is no zodiac year of the absent father

The year after you stopped answering my calls

... was the Chinese Year of the Wood Horse. The year of the plane crashes. The International Year of Small Island Developing States.

The year my mother found a lump in her left breast and there was nobody to tell because

YOU

were somewhere in Cambodia, you were finding yourself, and when I called around to try and find you too I realised that I had misplaced your name.

Then it was

... the International Year of Soil and of Light, and they found pieces of the plane from last year on an island called Reunion, and still ***you*** were out there looking for you.

We had taken to calling The Lump *Gloria*, and she swelled and shrank and then kept shrinking.

She was smaller than a grape and we were trying to make her more of a raisin, and my mother kept asking if I had anyone to talk to about it all. I tried to reach you with messages in bottles, and then I felt guilty for flinging my thought-trash into the sea.

When we finally made it to

... the year that Western reality broke, we were in the sign of the Metal Monkey. It was the International Year of Global Understanding.

Gloria had packed her bags and left, and got both my mother's breasts in the divorce. There was no lawyer that could have changed the outcome.

I had forgotten all about *you*, and I got up on my imaginary stage and said so at every opportunity, and bartenders and cab drivers and Tesco cashiers all asked 'who?' and I said '*exactly.*'

My mother, with her new body and her scars and her health-despite-it-all, claimed not to need me anymore. She packed me a lunch and I paddled out to sea in a second-hand canoe, trusting the blue marble to roll right and deliver me to you.

I'm running late, I guess. It's only because I stopped to meet myself in some city along the way.

roadside jam

Jams £2.50
Leave the money in the box on the gate
– Bob

I could not find the box you were talking about so I left a note under the piccalilli
– Linda

Jams £2.50
Leave the money in the box on the gate, please do not put under the piccalilli or any jars as I won't find it in time
– Bob

Sorry to hear about the note theft. I still can't find this box so I left the coins in the flowerpot this time.
– Linda

Jams £2.50
Leave the money in the box on the gate, not under any jars or flowerpots, which I have many.
– Bob

Have you thought of putting a sign up to show where this box is?
– Linda

Jams £2.50
Leave the money in the box on the gate, which I have indicated with the large sign which says "Money Box this way".
– Bob

Thanks for the sign Bob. Do you sell anything else or just jams?
– Linda

Jams £2.50
Leave the money in the box on the gate, as indicated by the sign. Eggs also available for £2 a box but please ring this number and I will bring them down for you. I can't risk the vandalism again.
– Bob

I tried ringing the number but got voicemail.

– Linda

Jams £2.50

Leave the money in the box on the gate, as indicated by the sign. Eggs also available for £2 a box but please ring this number and I will bring them down for you. Please bear in mind I am only home between 6pm and 10pm.

– Bob

Where do you go after 10pm?

– Linda

Jams £2.50

Leave the money in the box on the gate, as indicated by the sign. Eggs also available for £2 a box but please ring this number and I will bring them down for you. Please bear in mind I am only home and awake between 6pm and 10pm.

– Bob

That's less exciting. I liked to imagine you were a normal jammaker by day and catburglar by night.

– Linda

Jams £2.50

Leave the money in the box on the gate, as indicated by the sign. Eggs also available for £2 a box but please ring this number and I will bring them down for you. I go to bed at 10pm so will not answer the phone after then, because I am a normal person and not a catburglar although I imagine if I was a catburglar I would not disclose this publicly.

– Bob

I hope your wife is not too disturbed by this obvious catburglaring you're doing.

– Linda

Jams £2.50
Leave the money in the box on the gate, as indicated by the sign. Eggs also available for £2 a box but please ring this number and I will bring them down for you. Please bear in mind I live alone so you may have to ring more than once.

– Bob

Alone eh? You know I've been wondering how to make jam myself.

– Linda

Jams £2.50
Leave the money in the box on the gate, as indicated by the sign. Eggs also available for £2 a box but please ring this number and I will bring them down for you. I can also offer one-on-one jam making classes.

– Bob

How do I arrange one of these classes?

– Linda

Jams £2.50
Leave the money in the box on the gate, as indicated by the sign. Eggs also available for £2 a box but please ring this number and I will bring them down for you. I can also offer one-on-one jam making classes. You have my number already.

– Bob

Bob and Linda's Jams £2.50
Leave the money in the box on the gate, as indicated by the sign.

hokey cokey

You put your whole self in
your whole self out
in
out
in
out

Where's dad?

We haven't finished

You put your whole self in
your whole self out
in
out

Where's dad?

DAD

She looks at her circle of friends, dwindling, shifty, Milky Way insides smeared on the corner of Sarah's mouth, party hat askew.

You put your whole self in
your whole self out
in

in

in, I said in

But they've gone. Well they've gone apart from Sarah, Sarah licks some milky white crust into her mouth and smiles meekly.

She hops

in

out

she out

or I out

I out
she in

I in

I out

she out

in

out

in

out

get out

Sarah get out

get out of the circle.

She looks at Sarah, lips quivering, remnants of the dried malty foam gathering in the left crease.

Sarah stares back reproachfully

then disappears into the ground.

They always disappear into the ground. She doesn't want them to. She doesn't mean them to. But then they're gone.

You put your whole self in
your whole self out
in

DAD. DAD YOU SAID YOU WOULD THIS TIME.

She suddenly notices dad is busy kissing Karen in the corner.

She wishes with all her heart Sarah would come back in. But she's out.

Gone for good, kaput, nada, in absentia, auf wiedersehen, byebye, ciao for now but forever, gone with the wind, neither here nor there, zero, down the drain, MIA, been there done that, indefinite leave, no more, fucked off, a whisper on the breeze, out.

I suppose I did that.

She supposes she did that, she thinks. She could do that sometimes, disappear them. She wishes she'd disappeared the party hats too. They look weird on the floor like that. Eleven of them.

She looks over to check Dad is still wearing his.

In
out
in
out
shake it all about

And she does. She really shakes, she shakes and she shakes and she shakes, hoping Dad will stop kissing Karen like that, Karen's 71, Karen can't even join in anyway because of her osteoarthritis, but Dad keeps kissing Karen,

shake it all about
shake it all about
shake it all about
shake it all about
shake it all about
it's no good.
I'm not shaking good enough.

She takes a breath

In
out
in
out
shake it all about

And she does, she really shakes, she shakes, and she shakes and she shakes, much better this time, much shakier, hoping dad will stop moving on Karen like that, it's time to hop in Dad, but Dad keeps moving around on Karen like that,

shake it all about
shake it all about
shake it
I can't.

She decides she can't. She can, she could keep going, but she can't, if you know what she means.

Dad is blurry now.

He gets blurry sometimes, it probably means her mum is near

Oh hi mum, do you want to-

Dad has definitely become more nebulous than usual

Oh hi mum, would you like to-

Dad has almost completely spilled out of his outline

Oh hi mum, I was wondering if you-

Her mum takes Karen's walking stick and throws it out the window. Smash. She should have opened the window first. At least it wasn't a very nice window.

You put your whole self in
Ow that's glass, that's a huge piece of glass sticking out of my foot, ow that actually really hurts, MUM! Actually don't worry, it's fine, the queue at casualty is long, I don't need to go. I promise,

she promises as she instinctively feels the scar under her chin.

And the scar under her knee.

It doesn't really matter when they're in places you can't see anyway. And it's always a bloody long wait at A&E and mum doesn't have time because dad's dissolving.

Do you want some cake?

Her mum stalks away in floods of tears, wincing as she treads on six out of the eleven pointy party hats. She feels awful for being so selfish, of course her mum doesn't want cake, there's blood on it. Now she knows how Sarah felt, she was only trying to be a friend, she really shouldn't have disappeared her, she wishes Sarah were there now. In

in

out

nope, Dad's still kissing Karen

She thinks about how her Dad is still kissing Karen while thinking about how to try and not think about her Dad kissing Karen.

Suddenly her Dad stands up with a massive laugh but somehow her heart isn't lifted by the bellowing sound like it used to be. Maybe because he's now pixelated.

Dad, why are you pixelated?

He shoves a can of diet coke zero extra lite into her hand

In

out

in

out

Wow he's actually doing it

out

in

out

in

No, that's the wrong way round

in/out

out/in

in/out

out/in

No, Dad you have to do it the same order as me

in
out
in out in out shake it all about bout bout out out out
out
out
out

out.

Dad?

Where is her Dad, she wonders.

Mum?

Where is her mum, she wonders.

She notes Karen is there though. Trying to leave but tumbling over horribly with every gammy step now that her walking stick is gone. It's painful to watch.

I should help her

She doesn't help her.

She looks behind the sofa then pauses. She looks under the rug then pauses. She doesn't remember agreeing to switch to Hide and Seek, but at least she might find them soon and then they can go back to the circle.

She looks behind the TV then pauses. She looks at her watch and realises it's now next year. Karen is a bit closer to the door but it's now pretty chilly because snow is coming in through the broken window in an unseasonably cold April. It strikes her as a bit unfair as well as a lot cold to leave her looking for so long, but then again she was never a very good seeker.

She finds a cheese biscuit on the floor under a piece of glass and nibbles in silence, cutting her tongue on a hidden shard.

Ow tha's glasth, tha's a huchge pieche of glasth sthtickih ou' o' my tunng, ow, MUM!

MUM!

She's just about to apologise for calling her mum over when she realises her mum's not coming over.

Oh well, in a way it's ok, she's now learnt to regrow damaged cells anyway. And if there's anywhere you can't see a scar it's on your tongue.

She decides she needs more thermal energy than Hide and Seek is offering

You put your whole self in
your whole self

but it dawns on her that Dad's probably out for good this time. He's had 11 months, 9 days, 17 hours and 26 minutes to hop back in. And he usually comes inside when it's cold.

She looks on top of the bookshelf then pauses.

The party hats are gone.

She can't tell if she disappeared him or he disappeared her. He did teach her that after all, she thought.

He did teach me that after all.
I wish I never learnt that trick.

POETRY
18-23

refraction

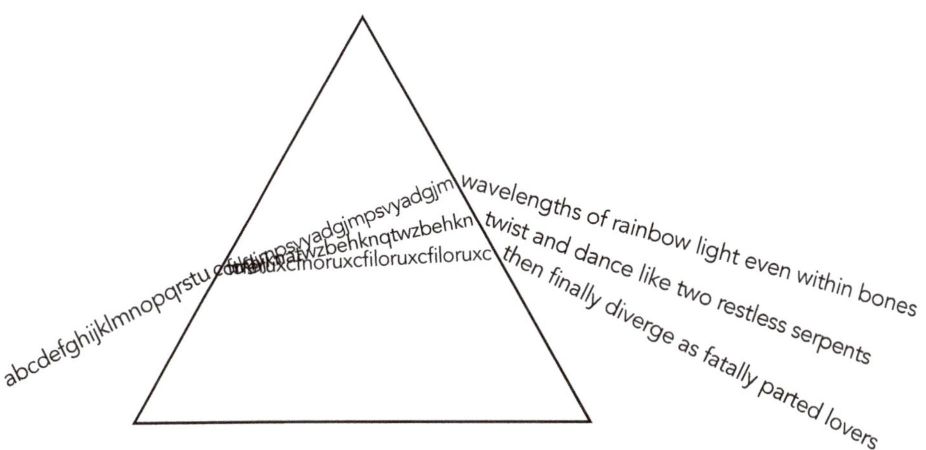
abcdefghijklmnopqrstu
adgjmpsvyadgjm
wzbehknqtwzbehkn
filoruxcfiloruxc
wavelengths of rainbow light even within bones
twist and dance like two restless serpents
then finally diverge as fatally parted lovers

crosswords

ALIENATION
NOT
THESE
LETTERS
BEING
DISOBEDIENT
SHARING SPACE
FIGHTING
CRAMMING
OVERWHELMINGLY
ARE
AND
IS
WORDS
RULES
WHAM
IMMORTAL
AGAINST
ORDER
CREATE
RIGHT
REGARDLESS
UNLIKE
IF
EXPECTED
WRONG
ENOUGH
DEFINE
END
DEAD
CONSECUTIVE
OF
CAUSES
NUMBERS
BUT
THAT
SQUAR
SYMBOL
SEE
INTERRUPTED
rules are the reason why
set
their existence whereas
True rules establish
sense.
indifferent
and
nonsense
principled
away from
time
warping
iagonally

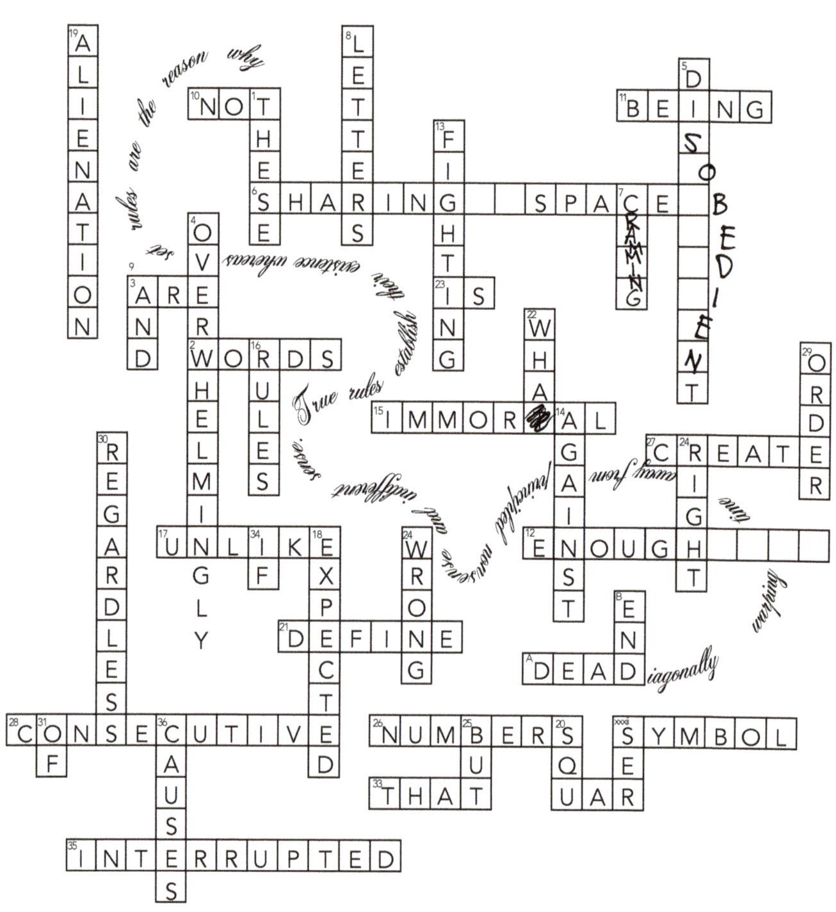

schiehallion

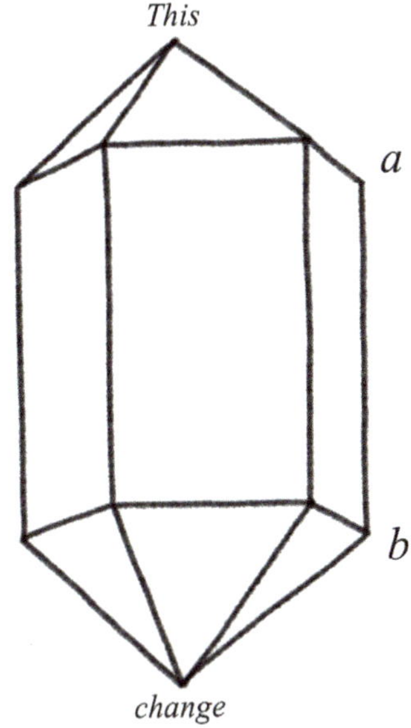

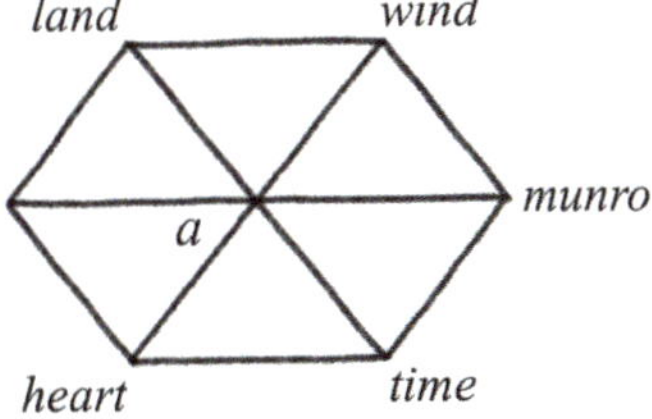

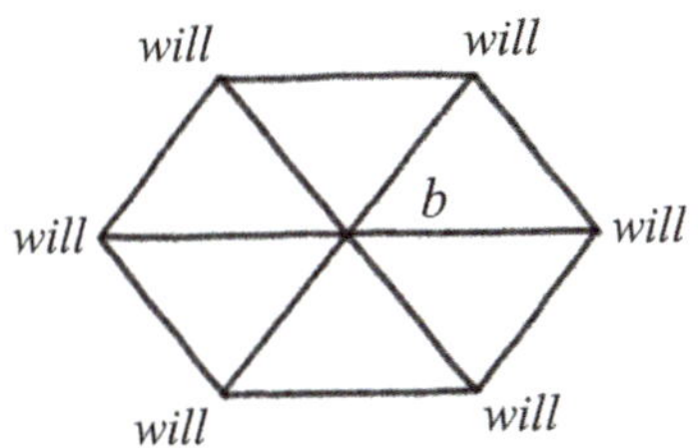

Figure 1: Quartz crystal, poem

round-a-bout

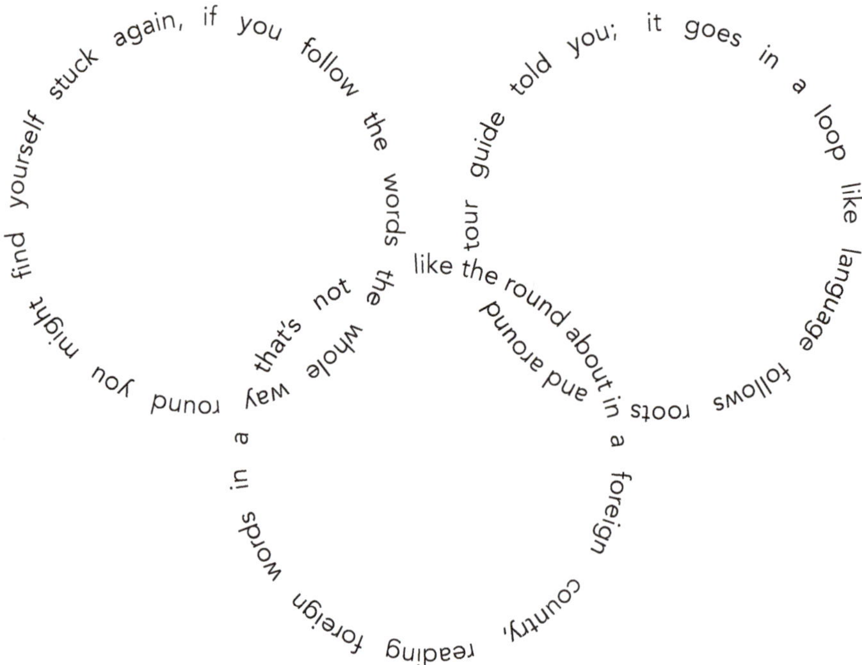

find yourself stuck again, if you follow the words the tour guide told you; it goes in a loop like language follows roots
and around like the round about in a foreign country, reading foreign words in a
way that's not the whole way round you might

POETRY 24-30

woman in a tub by edgar degas

faqs about concrete

To be of a city
is to ask questions of concrete:

Q. if you're so real
then why does it take till the
third dictionary definition
to find what you're made of?

To be of a city
is to ask questions of concrete:

Q. if you're so permanent
why don't I recognise you
from one week to the next?

To be of a city
is to ask questions of concrete:

Q. if you're so fixed
when will you stop looking
like a patient on an operating table
waiting for their ribs to grow together?

Q. if you know outright
what can I do
that will change your mind?

if you're so solid
where does the feeling of
moving beneath my feet come from?

On the face of it
a concrete poem is just
a poem in which the visual form is used to convey meaning...

on the face of concrete
what meaning doesn't get washed off eventually?

To be of a city
is to ask questions of concrete,

so try:
Q. if you're already all set
what is left to make handprints
or
write our names in now?

how to fall in love: an ode to

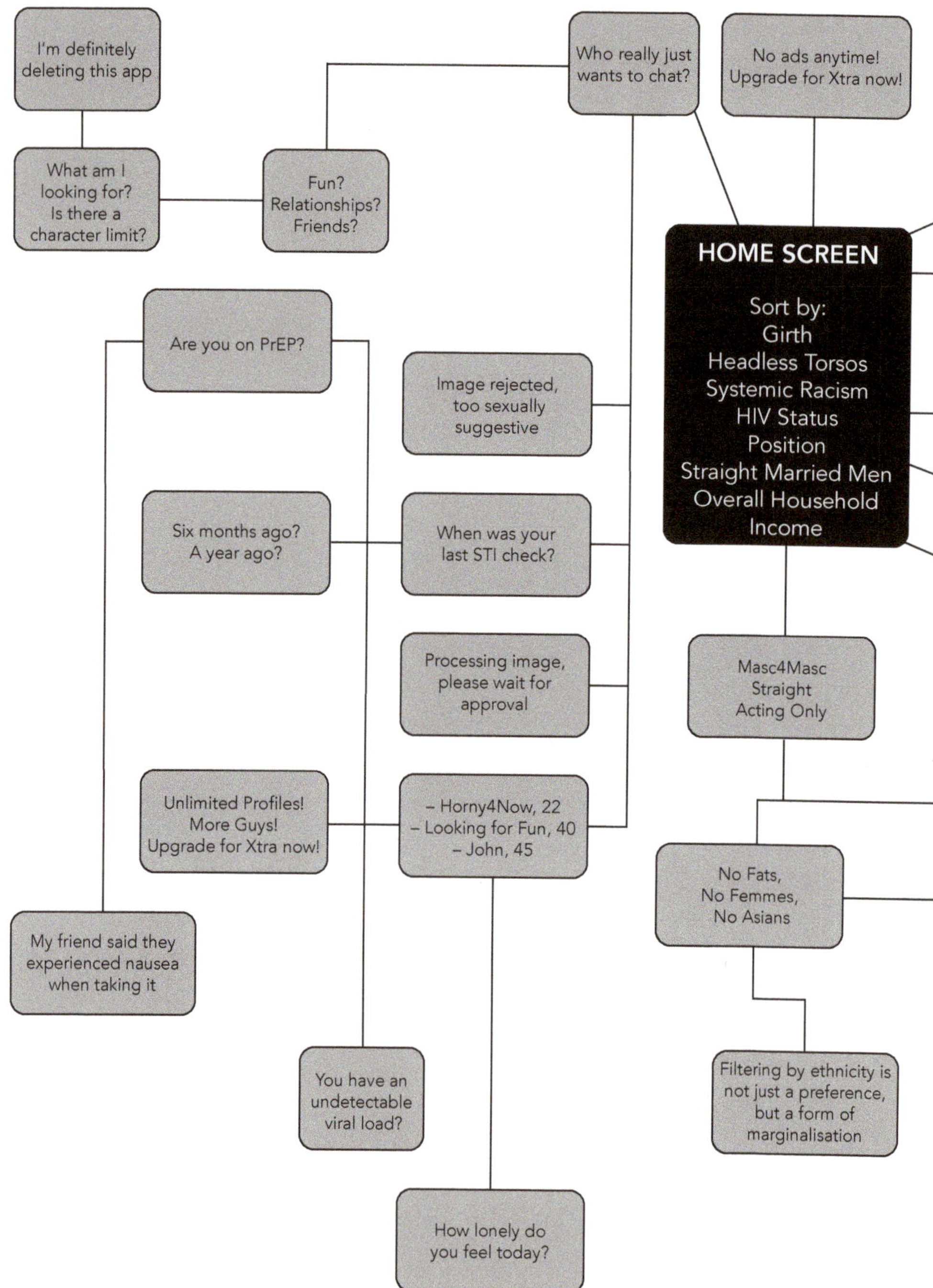

dating in the 21st century

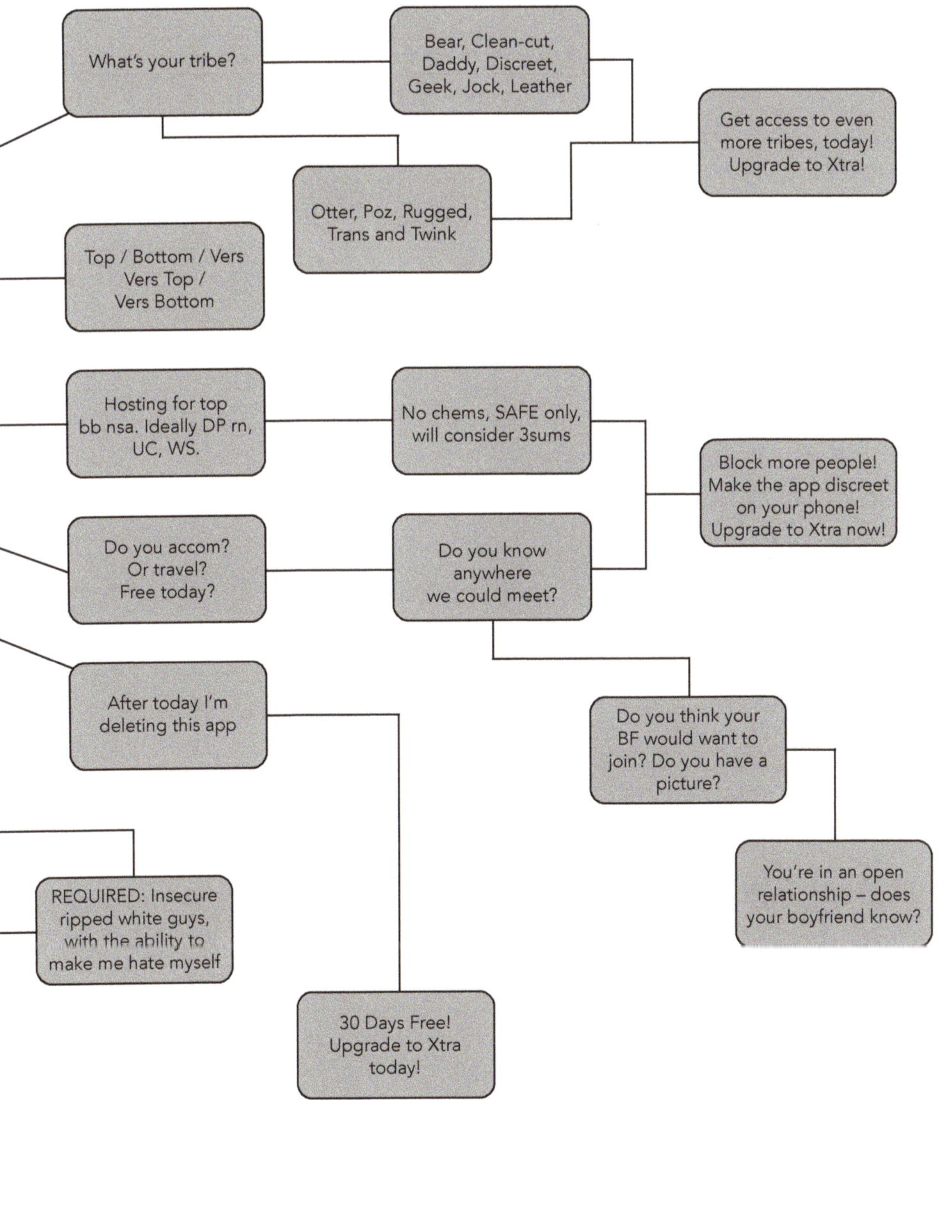

I think I'm in love

architexture

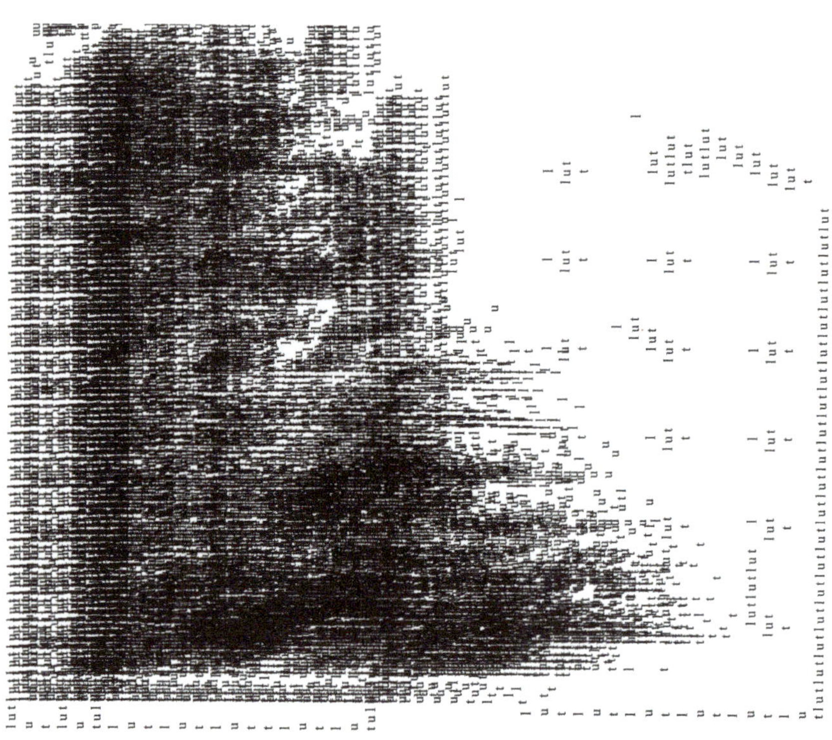

2020 shortlisted writers

Chloe Dyett

Charles Nurick

Gisella Doulton

Scott Barclay

Isaac Somerville

Eve Allin

Marie-Gabrielle Gallard

Aidan Smith

Allie Kerper

Siobhan Dunlop

David Bond

Declan Lloyd

Emily Fisher

Lucy C. Hulton

Belinda Bradley

Chastity Von Trapp

John Reid

Mehar Anaokar

Niamh Jerrie-Haran

Rachel Oyawale

partners

the 87 press

comma press

fly on the wall

Story
Machine
Productions

www.ingramcontent.com/pod-product-compliance
Ingram Content Group UK Ltd.
Pitfield, Milton Keynes, MK11 3LW, UK
UKHW062313290726
14090UKWH00018B/1050

9 781838 096007